T0207765

Make Your Bible Class Meaningful

Make Your Bible Class Meaningful

A Guide for Teachers of
Adult Bible Classes

Stephanie R. Moss

WESTBOW
PRESS*
A DIVISION OF THOMAS NELSON
& ZONDERVAN

All Scripture quotations, unless otherwise indicated, are taken from the Holy Bible, New International Version®, NIV®. Copyright ©1973, 1978, 1984, 2011 by Biblica, Inc.™ Used by permission of Zondervan. All rights reserved worldwide. www.zondervan.com The "NIV" and "New International Version" are trademarks registered in the United States Patent and Trademark Office by Biblica, Inc.

Scripture quotations marked KJV are taken from the King James Version of the Bible.

Scripture quotations marked ESV are from the ESV® Bible (The Holy Bible, English Standard Version®), copyright © 2001 by Crossway, a publishing ministry of Good News Publishers. Used by permission. All rights reserved.

WestBow Press books may be ordered through booksellers or by contacting:

WestBow Press
A Division of Thomas Nelson & Zondervan
1663 Liberty Drive
Bloomington, IN 47403
www.westbowpress.com
1 (866) 928-1240

ISBN: 978-1-9736-3004-3 (sc)
ISBN: 978-1-9736-3003-6 (e)

Print information available on the last page.

WestBow Press rev. date: 08/14/2018

For Mom, Kim, Janice, and Sandee

*Thank you for your encouragement,
honest feedback, and fervent prayers.*

Contents

Preface

What a delight it has been to serve in the field of education for over 30 years! It would take countless hours to share the many stories of lessons I have learned throughout my career as both a teacher and trainer. I have learned much about how to construct and teach a lesson, how to engage learners, how to build community, and which strategies and activities to use to make lessons meaningful so outcomes are met and concepts are remembered. Even though I had years of formal training, I learned many of my lessons the hard way—through trial and error as I engaged in the process of teaching. I thankfully acknowledge the talented colleagues, school leaders, mentors, researchers, educational consultants, and trainers who showed me the way. The resources, information, and feedback they provided made all the difference in my teaching success.

Through it all, I learned that good teaching always begins with a committed instructor, yet the effective transfer of knowledge takes a special set of skills and is often more than a notion!

Fortunately, the skills needed for effective teaching can be successfully acquired with a little guidance and practice. This guidebook was written to support the efforts of individuals who teach an adult Bible class in their church or another setting. Within these pages, I present information gained from the critical lessons I learned over my lifetime as a public school teacher, staff developer, educational consultant, and Bible class facilitator. I hope the tips shared in this book help make your teaching assignment a bit easier and assist you in becoming a more confident and skilled instructor. Like most Bible teachers, you know your content; this resource simply outlines some of the tasks you must undertake and the various elements that must be in place if your Bible class is to be a successful one. I commend you for the commitment you have made to Christian education and pray you will have the most rewarding teaching experience possible. May you receive fresh blessings as you share biblical truths and touch the lives of those you teach forever.

In Christ,

Stephanie R. Moss

Introduction

So Christ himself gave the apostles, the prophets,
the evangelists, the pastors and teachers,
to equip his people for works of service, so
that the body of Christ may be built up.
Ephesians 4:11–12

Christian education plays a significant role in strengthening the modern-day church and in equipping twenty-first century disciples for outreach and ministry. The success of a church's educational ministry is greatly influenced by the teachers who interact with learners week after week, so having skilled teachers who are knowledgeable and organized—and who know how to engage students—is critical.

Sometimes Bible teachers have a background in education and are quite familiar with the teaching and learning process. More often than not, individuals bestowed with the honor of teaching work in other fields and may have no idea of where to begin or what to do with a classroom full of students. This may be especially true for those assigned to teach a class of adult learners.

If you are a brand-new Bible teacher—or even if you have been teaching for years—the tips shared in this book will assist you in refining your instructional processes so the adult learners you serve get the most out of their interactions with you. Because most Bible classes provide only a short period of time for you to be with class members each week, it is important to carefully consider what you will do during the moments you spend together. A top priority is to make your instruction meaningful and engaging so it impacts learners and equips them with the knowledge and skills needed to enhance their day-to-day walk with God.

In this book, you will find suggestions to help you be the very best Bible teacher possible. Carefully apply the ideas shared within these pages, and you are sure to have a productive and enriching teaching experience.

In general, the work you will be held accountable for in teaching your class may be divided into these four categories:

1) preparing for your class
2) promoting your class to others

3) engaging your learners
4) reflecting and reporting on your work

This guidebook provides information on each of these topics and a few others. Review the entire book, or use the table of contents to zero in on the topics of greatest interest or need. Adapt the ideas to fit your teaching context and personal preferences.

Remember, teaching is hard work! You will need to reflect on your work often, and revise your strategies and techniques in order to continually refine your craft. The ideas shared here will help you get started. Get ready—you are on your way to teaching success!

Preparing for Your Class

Commit to the LORD whatever you do,
and he will establish your plans.
Proverbs 16:3

Serving in the role of Bible teacher is one of the most important volunteer assignments you will ever undertake. Ask any teacher you know, and he or she will tell you—teaching is challenging work! The good news is that it is also very fulfilling. You will find you will learn just as much as your students and create memories that will last a lifetime. Whether you are hosting a class in your home or workplace, serving in prison ministry, or teaching a weekly class at your place of worship, your responsibilities will pretty much be the same. Approaching the work with the same professionalism and energy you would commit to a salaried position is a key in carrying out this important work successfully.

In addition to the time you spend with class members, your teaching assignment will include many other responsibilities that must be attended to in order for your class to run smoothly. You will begin some of these tasks long before you set foot in your classroom and continue to work on them throughout the course of your instruction.

If you are reading this book, you have probably already prayerfully committed to a teaching assignment and have asked the key questions needed to begin the work. Your upfront considerations may have included questions such as these:

- *When does the class meet?*
- *What is the length of the teaching assignment?*
- *Who is the audience and what are their needs?*
- *How many students can I expect?*
- *What teaching materials are available for use?*
- *Is this a new or existing class?*
- *What outcomes are expected?*
- *Is there a budget to cover supplies and resources?*
- *Whom should I contact if I have questions or need support?*

Now that these questions have been answered, you are ready to begin taking action to prepare for your class. As you move forward, keep in mind the steps you will take are not linear. Though it makes sense to begin with prayer and consecration, you will find some tasks overlap and many will be carried out repeatedly during your teaching assignment.

Engage in Prayer and Consecration

Your success as a Bible teacher will depend not only on what you do when you are engaging with participants, but also on the steps you take long before the start of your first class. This means time must be consistently devoted to the ongoing duties of teaching.

One critical commitment to make upfront is preparing spiritually and mentally for the important work you will do. Your daily devotional time will take on new meaning as you seek God's guidance regarding instructional strategies, topics, and activities to meet participants' special needs and interests.

Prayer will be an ongoing part of your duties as a teacher. Through times of prayer and study, you will gain the wisdom needed for the work and will receive strength to persevere in times of challenge.

Set aside time to pray for the overall success of your class and for your prospective students. Also pray for your skill as a teacher and for the lessons you will share each week. If you regularly engage in the spiritual discipline of fasting, consider conducting a fast on behalf of this important work. Consult your physician prior to beginning a fast to make sure there are no health risks.

Seeking God's guidance will increase your effectiveness as a teacher and ensure your efforts are an acceptable, living sacrifice for Him. A class clothed in prayer is more likely to succeed. Make prayer a priority; it will greatly enhance your instruction.

Determine the Curriculum

Deciding what you will teach is a key task at the start of your teaching assignment. Sometimes your curriculum or instructional materials will be selected for you. For example, your church may use a particular set of study guides for all of its adult Sunday school classes. In other cases, you will have the flexibility of selecting the materials on your own. Occasionally, you may be required to design your lessons from scratch. Whatever your situation, give yourself ample time to develop materials or to conduct a thorough search—the resources you utilize will be the heart of your instruction.

Selecting Class Materials

If you are responsible for selecting class materials, begin by thinking about the needs of your target audience and the outcomes you desire. Also think about resources currently available in the marketplace that could guide or supplement your instruction. A trip to your local Christian bookstore and an in-depth Web search are definitely in order.

As you conduct your search, note study materials that seem to be a good fit for your group. Select topics that align with current church initiatives or those that might be of most interest to your target audience. If class members must purchase their own study materials, carefully consider the cost to ensure that fees are aligned with what people are willing or able to pay.

After you have identified several prospective resources, narrow your search by seeking feedback from church leaders and a few individuals in your target audience. This input will assist you in making your final selection.

Once your final selection has been made, check with your ministry leader to find out the process for purchasing the resources. Your organization may obtain the materials for class members to buy on-site at the church bookstore or on the first day of class. This often allows the materials to be purchased at a discounted rate and eases the burden an online purchase or a trip to a bookstore may cause for some class members.

Creating Lessons on Your Own

If you are faced with the challenge of creating lessons on your own, start early so you have sufficient time to complete this labor-intensive work. You will need to have an idea of what you are trying to accomplish and what knowledge and skills you would like participants to gain.

A helpful technique for getting started is to identify a central theme or topic. Once the focal topic has been identified, connect all lessons to this theme. Consider including some or all of the following components in each lesson you develop:

> **Title:** *What will the lesson be called?*
> **Purpose/Goal of Lesson:** *What is the overall focus of the lesson?*
> **Key Questions:** *What key questions will be considered and answered during the study?*
> **Learning Outcomes:** *What should participants know or be able to do by the end of the lesson?*

Scripture References: *Which Bible verses support the lesson content?*

Introduction of Topic: *How will the topic of study be introduced in order to engage your audience?*

Discussion and Scripture Reading: *What, specifically, will be discussed? How do these ideas relate to the chosen Bible verses?*

Summary of Key Ideas: *How will you close out the lesson so participants review and remember the ideas shared?*

Life Application Challenge: *What will you ask participants to do to apply what they have learned in their daily lives?*

In order to stay focused on the overall goals you have for your class, try to have all lessons developed by the time your first class begins. This will ensure lessons are designed as a cohesive unit with solid connections from the first class to the final one.

Note materials you might need for each lesson and identify specific activities to be implemented. Keep detailed copies of the lessons you create so they can be refined and reused when needed.

Plan and Study Lessons

Do your best to present yourself to God as one
approved, a worker who does not need to be ashamed
and who correctly handles the word of truth.
2 Timothy 2:15

Once you have begun your mental and spiritual preparation and have selected or developed your curriculum, it is time to become more familiar with your course materials. Set aside a regular time each week to prepare for your class. You will be much more likely to enjoy the commitment you have made if you do not have the added stress of rushing to complete last-minute tasks the night before—or worse yet—on the day of class! To avoid such stressors, complete as many tasks as you can as far ahead of time as possible.

If you have designed the class curriculum on your own, you will already be familiar with the content. Thus, refining and adding depth to your lessons may be all that is required. If you are using purchased resources, more time will be needed to familiarize yourself with the materials. In most cases, it will be essential to set aside two or more hours each week to study the lesson, conduct background research, prepare materials, make follow-up contacts, and engage in class-related prayer and meditation. Make prep time part of your weekly routine by designating a regular time and place for these activities.

Some churches hold regular meetings for Bible teachers where weekly lessons are reviewed and discussed. Such meetings provide an opportunity to clarify personal interpretations and to ask questions prior to class. If this is the case at your church, try to regularly attend these important meetings. This will give you an opportunity to interact with other teachers and to share and receive feedback on the ideas you have for your lesson. Such activities will greatly enhance your instructional effectiveness.

As you study each lesson, think about enhancements you might make to meet the needs of your group. Could additional resources be used to make the lesson more engaging? Is there a handout or prop which might make the content more memorable? Most purchased study materials will need a bit of tweaking and the addition of your creative ideas to make them more suitable for your specific audience. To be most effective, additional resources must be carefully selected and align with core materials and learning outcomes. Use extra resources sparingly to further clarify ideas or to add an additional perspective on a topic.

Prepare Recordkeeping Materials

Another matter to consider before the start of your first class is recordkeeping. This task is often overlooked, but it is a critical one. The information you gather will be a valuable resource as you reflect on your work and plan for future classes.

The first day of class is a great time to gather baseline information from each participant. This information might include:

⇒ name
⇒ phone number
⇒ email address
⇒ birth month and day
⇒ membership status (member or visitor)

Participants might write this information on an index card, or you can create a sign-in sheet for this purpose. Another alternative is to collect this information digitally. Check to see if your organization has a platform in place to assist with the collection and maintenance of participant data. Attendance apps and other free or low-cost resources are also available for use with electronic devices.

When collecting personal information, be sure to tell participants how you will use it. Typically, the information you collect should not be shared with others. It should be used by you and only for purposes related to class. If you want to develop and distribute the class roster to all participants, explain the guidelines for use and give class members an opportunity to be removed from the "public" list. Use the information you collect to keep learners abreast of important news throughout the class. You might also use it to personalize the learning experience with special acknowledgements on birthdays or at other times of your choosing.

If you manually collect participant information, it will make your work easier if you compile all of the names and accompanying data into one document. Having all of the contact information in one place will allow you to easily monitor attendance and help you stay abreast of attendance milestones. During each class period, a sign-in sheet might be used to record the names of those in attendance. After each class, this information can be noted on the compiled document or entered into the electronic system so you can see at a glance who has attended consistently and who has been out for a while and needs to be contacted.

Keep your records accurate and up-to-date by reviewing them regularly and noting changes immediately after each class. Staying organized and quickly noting changes will make this task less burdensome.

As you gather information about the adult learners in your class, remember they will also be interested in learning more about you. Class members may wonder about your personal background or what qualifies you to teach the class. Build in time at the start of your first class to share a little about yourself and your spiritual journey. Be brief and maintain a spirit of humility. Depending on the length and nature of your class, you might create a brief bio and share it with class members. This will give them information about you without taking up valuable class time. Make a conscious effort to provide opportunities for your class members to learn more about you as your class progresses.

Keeping a record of who attends your class and disclosing information about yourself will help you get to know participants and increase your credibility as a teacher. Such efforts will go a long way in creating a welcoming environment that supports the open dialogue conducive to learning.

Plan Ahead

As your ideas for your class begin to take form, you will need to handle logistics such as reserving a classroom, informing support staff of the desired room arrangement, and determining if snacks are allowed or needed. Your ministry leader may be in charge of these items and should be your first point of contact. During this initial planning stage, it is also time to begin thinking about tasks that will be implemented throughout or near the end of your class.

Feedback

One task to think about is how you will gather feedback from participants so you will know what adjustments you should make to your class as you move forward. For ongoing classes, feedback might be gathered at designated times during the year. For shorter classes (i.e., a six- to eight-week class), a feedback survey may be implemented at the end of your course of study.

You will need to determine how you will gather this information. A hard-copy or electronic survey may be in order. Whatever your choice, begin thinking about your feedback survey early in your preparations since it may prove challenging to find time to complete this critical task once your class begins. Additional information related to this topic will be shared later in this guidebook.

Guest Speakers

If you plan to invite guest speakers to class, now is the time to inform them of tentative dates and topics. Review your course content to determine which lessons might be enhanced with a special speaker. Set tentative dates with prospective guests and send a follow-up email as you get closer to the day of the event. If required, obtain approval from your leader prior to making contact with speakers to avoid misunderstandings and confusion.

Celebration

There is still one more thing to think about. It is also time to begin preliminary planning for the end-of-course celebration. Though the plans for your celebration will evolve as your class progresses, early in your planning is a good time to begin thinking about how you will acknowledge participants' hard work. This might include setting a date for the celebration, reserving a room or other location, outlining a budget, and determining special recognitions you would like to include as part of celebratory activities.

Even though it may be too early to finalize plans, giving thought to upcoming tasks such as securing guests, gathering feedback, and celebrating accomplishments will help future activities run more smoothly. You will discover that time will pass swiftly once the class is in session.

Enlist Support

Two are better than one, because they
have a good return for their labor:
If either of them falls down, one can help the other up.
Ecclesiastes 4:9-10a

After reading the information above, you may wonder if you are cut out for all of the work involved in teaching. If this is the case, now is a great time to enlist a team of supporters who will help you throughout your teaching assignment.

Teaching Assistant

Begin by identifying someone to serve as your assistant. Though this person may not regularly teach lessons, he or she can be a wonderful resource with whom to toss around ideas, help with record keeping, substitute in case of your absence, or to provide moral support and ongoing encouragement.

If you are able to work with a partner, arrange times when you can meet to plan and pray together. Meetings do not always have to be face-to-face. Conference calls, emails, and other virtual options often work well for discussing class needs or for joining together in prayer.

Take time to determine the parameters for your work together. Be straightforward about your needs and the role you would like your assistant to play. Following are a few things you might discuss with your assistant.

- *Will he or she help plan and teach lessons or just provide administrative support?*
- *Is he or she expected to attend every class?*
- *What time should he or she arrive?*
- *What ongoing responsibilities would you like him or her to carry out?*
- *Is he or she expected to support class activities with monetary donations?*

Communicate openly and touch base often to make sure there are no misunderstandings about roles and responsibilities. Maintaining an ongoing dialogue with two-way feedback will prevent or minimize any difficulties that may arise.

If you are unable to assign a permanent assistant, you can enlist help from participants who attend the class on a regular basis. You will be able to easily identify prospective candidates—class members who have good attendance, participate in discussions, or who tend to linger after class has been dismissed. One or more of these individuals may be honored to serve as a helper and can be depended upon for the support you need. Be thoughtful about your selection and keep a record of who helps so you can acknowledge these participants during the celebration or at some other time during class.

Prayer Team

If your organization has a prayer team, enlist their support to consistently cover your class in prayer. The prayer team might pray for the class in general and can also assist you in praying for ongoing concerns that may be submitted by class members each week. A request for prayer support might be made as you begin class preparations; then, identify a point person and determine the process you will use to submit prayer requests to him or her after each class. You will find comfort in knowing your class is being prayed for on a regular basis. This one action will greatly impact the success of your Bible class.

Family Members and Friends

Your family members and friends should also be made aware of your commitment so they will be on board to provide needed support. Let them know how much time you will need to prepare for your class and what adjustments you will make in your daily schedule to ensure quality time remains available for them. Also, explain the kinds of support you would like from them as your class progresses. Both family members and friends might be enlisted to pray on your behalf, to attend or help market the class, or to help prepare handouts and other materials. Having the support of those who know you best will mean a lot during the times of stress or challenge that are an inevitable part of the teaching and learning cycle. Encourage family members and friends to support your ongoing work.

Experienced Teachers

Finally, make an effort to connect with other individuals who have experience teaching adult Bible classes. These individuals will be able to give you first-hand information and can serve as helpful troubleshooters and confidants. Veteran teachers will also be able to share experiences and provide suggestions based on what has worked for them in the past. This type of feedback is invaluable since some aspects of teaching are learned only through hands-on experience.

Whatever you do, do not think you have to go it alone. Be proactive in seeking the help of others. As you depend on them for support, you will lighten your workload and be empowered to carry out your duties successfully.

Communicate with Leaders and Staff

As your class preparations progress, your ministry leader will be able to provide insight about important details related to your class. For example, should an offering be collected? Are snacks allowed? Is it okay to meet off site? Knowing the answers to these questions will help you make good decisions as you plan and implement class activities.

Be proactive in asking questions and in sharing highlights or challenges with the person designated to oversee your work. Make it a priority to touch base often to communicate relevant updates. This can be done informally during a casual contact or via phone or email. For more critical issues, a face-to-face meeting is desirable. For best results, check with your leader at the start of your commitment to see which communication mode works best for him or her. Also, find out how often he or she would like to receive ongoing updates.

In addition to communicating with your ministry leader, there are several other staff members with whom you'll want to connect early on— the administrative assistant and the custodian or building operator. You are likely to need the help of these individuals on numerous occasions throughout your teaching assignment. Developing a good rapport upfront will make it easier to ask for help when you need it. Talk with them directly to determine the procedures for things such as entering the building, copying materials, obtaining supplies, maintaining the cleanliness of your classroom, and submitting paperwork for reimbursement of class-related purchases.

The support systems you put in place will play a big part in your teaching success. Stay connected, and seek the support of others to do your job well.

Promoting Your Class to Others

The voice of him that crieth in the wilderness,
Prepare ye the way of the LORD,
make straight in the desert a highway for our God.
Isaiah 40:3 (KJV)

As you prepare for your class, it is also time to begin telling others about the upcoming learning opportunity. Such efforts will help ensure the hard work you have completed during preparation is not in vain—you definitely want to have some students in class on the first day! The approach you take will depend on the audience you are targeting and the processes used in your organization. Use methods that inform, inspire, and capture the attention of prospective participants.

Inform Your Audience

Even if your church or organization has a process in place for sharing information with others, *you* must be the driving force that ensures your target audience is informed about your class.

Find out what is commonly done in your setting. Identify processes and tools already in place that could help you easily get the word out to others. To achieve the best results, use multiple avenues to communicate your message. Church announcements, flyers, email marketing, social media, and personal invitations are just a few great ways to spread the word about your class.

You may feel a bit hesitant to begin talking with others about the class when all of the details have not yet been finalized, but do not wait until everything is planned and ready to go before you begin sharing. Grab people's interest early and share additional details as they are solidified. This will help build anticipation and will also be a motivator for you as you continue with class preparations.

For best results, begin advertising your class four to six weeks in advance of the start date. Share information about your class in various ways and continue to do so as often as possible until the day class begins. Your prospective participants probably lead very busy lives, and some may need to hear (and see) the information multiple times and in multiple formats before they make a commitment to attend.

If your class meets year-round, select specific times of the year to market the class to others. Reach out to new members, and continually remind participants to bring a friend to class. An excellent time to reach out for new attendees is when special guests or activities are planned.

Extend Ongoing Invitations

Once your class has started, continue to extend invitations to others who fit your target audience. Expect new participants to join the group at any time and have a plan for how you will gather their contact information and quickly acquaint them with class routines. Having your class membership change continually may be a bit frustrating at first, but it is important to go out of your way to make new class members feel welcome and a part of the group. Your assistant or other support person will be a big help in these situations.

New class members and sudden schedule changes are an inevitable part of the teaching and learning cycle and should be expected. Above all, remain positive and be flexible while keeping the goal of your instruction in mind. Remember, the Holy Spirit is in charge. He will send whomever He desires at the appointed time. Rest in the assurance that late arrivers have joined the group at the time designated by God. Go forth with the confidence that each participant is receiving what he or she needs at just the right moment.

Engaging Your Learners

I was glad when they said unto me, Let
us go into the house of the LORD.
Psalm 122:1 (KJV)

As your first day of teaching approaches, you will probably find yourself thinking about what might actually happen once participants arrive in your classroom. Continue in prayer as you review your first lesson, and move forward knowing you are well-prepared for your first day of class. It is now time to set the stage for your instruction.

Arrange the Room

The room arrangement you select for your class will vary depending on the size of the room, the activities you have planned, and the number of people in your group. Determine in advance how you want the chairs or tables arranged. This task may be carried out by other staff but, sometimes, you will be responsible for taking care of it yourself.

If the size of your group is large, you may decide to have rows of chairs. If the group is smaller and more intimate, a semicircle of chairs may be sufficient. Sometimes tables are also available. Think about the atmosphere you are trying to create, and arrange your room accordingly. All participants should have a clear view of you and any visual aids that will be used during class. Also, make sure you leave plenty of room for participants to enter and exit the learning space. If possible, arrange the seating so the entry door is located near the back of the classroom. This will prevent distractions if class members arrive after the designated start time.

Try out various seating arrangements and make adjustments until you find the ideal arrangement for the lessons you will be presenting. For best results, visit your room prior to the first day of class so you can determine what furniture is available. This will give you ample time to think about possibilities for the space provided. Occasionally change the arrangement you use to keep things fresh and exciting.

Create Ambiance

Preparing your classroom atmosphere for your time of worship will set the tone for what is to come. If appropriate, create ambiance by playing soft background music as participants enter. Find songs that relate to the current lesson, and you will begin ministering as soon as participants arrive. Use carefully chosen artifacts placed in strategic places to pique participants' interest and to focus their mind on the topic of discussion.

Depending on the time of day your class meets, you might consider making snacks available. If this is an acceptable practice in your teaching environment, select healthy snacks that allow for easy preparation and clean-up. Water, snack bars, fruit, nuts, or other healthy treats are often enough to create an atmosphere of hospitality. Because snacks and props sometimes distract learners from the true purpose of the lesson, you will need to be thoughtful when including them. Continuously observe the impact these items have on your participants and your instructional time, and make adjustments as needed.

Establish Norms

During your first few classes—and at other times when participants need to be reminded—discuss the norms you have set for your class. These are the expected ways of doing things in your classroom. Simple norms such as the ones below might be displayed for all to see and discussed briefly during the first session.

⇒ Begin and end on time
⇒ Participate actively
⇒ Respect the ideas of others
⇒ Get to know someone new
⇒ Maintain confidentiality

Explain what is meant by each statement and invite members of the class to add their own interpretations. Carve out time to discuss the norms and review them often. Each class member should be aware of the climate you would like to maintain in your classroom.

Share Information with Learners

Of the many tasks a teacher undertakes, often the most rewarding one is actually sharing information with learners. Make your class informative and engaging by having a regular routine and using a variety of teaching strategies.

Present Your Lesson

Capturing participants' attention at the start of your lesson will draw them in and get them focused on the topic of the day. You might pose a question, tell a story or ask participants to complete a brief reflective exercise. Once you have their attention, manage your lesson content and activities so participants stay engaged throughout the class period. Include special materials, technology, and outside resources to add excitement and interest to your class. When appropriate, you might:

- invite a special guest to share a testimony or to speak on a relevant topic.
- connect lesson content with a current event or a hot media topic.
- bring in a prop or show a video clip that relates to the topic of study.
- include dramatization, games, music or humor.

As you work with participants, think of yourself as a facilitator of learning rather than an expert scholar. Though you have put in many hours of study and may bring a great deal of knowledge and experience to the topic, your goal is to help class members make meaning through their own experiences and revelations. Your teaching approach must acknowledge and value the unique skills and experiences adult learners bring to the learning process. Make the sharing of ideas, opinions, and personal stories a natural part of your class. Also, build in time for questions and provide opportunities for discussion, debate, and reflection.

Since some participants may not feel comfortable sharing with the entire group, include opportunities for pairs or small groups to talk together. If space and time permit, you might occasionally include activities which require class members to move around so they can engage with classmates with whom they have not previously interacted.

In the beginning some class members may feel hesitant to contribute their ideas, but you should not feel compelled to speak if no one immediately responds when a question is posed. Most learners need time to formulate ideas before sharing a response. The moments of silence may seem a bit uncomfortable at first, but with a few moments of "wait time" participants will begin to open up in the warm setting of your classroom.

Use Various Teaching Roles

During the course of a lesson, you may take on many different teaching roles. These might include:

Presenter – sharing background information and highlighting key facts and definitions

Facilitator – clarifying thinking, keeping activities moving, directing the flow of conversation with guiding questions, challenging thinking with examples from the Bible, providing alternate examples for participants to think about

Storyteller – sharing short personal anecdotes or other true-to-life examples to support a concept

Coach – referring participants to supporting passages in the Bible or encouraging them to take an important next step to enhance their spiritual growth and development

You will need to fine tune your listening skills in order to adjust your style based on the information being presented. This will become second nature to you as you get to know participants and become more comfortable with the flow of instruction.

As you share information with participants, remember your teaching assignment is not a venue for you to show off your Bible knowledge or to highlight your spiritual encounters. Though you will naturally share personal anecdotes and stories, your main objective is to help participants expand their own knowledge. Growth will occur as class members share their thoughts and experiences and hear the ideas of others.

Manage Your Time

Look carefully then how you walk,
not as unwise but as wise,
making the best use of the time,
because the days are evil.
Ephesians 5:15-16 (ESV)

Managing your instructional time effectively will help ensure all course material is covered and that you have honored the time class members have committed to this endeavor. Good time management is needed during all phases of instruction to keep lessons on target and to help learners stay engaged and focused.

Before Class

Effective time management begins even before your class is in session. Whenever possible, arrive at least thirty minutes before the start of class. This will allow time to take care of last-minute details prior to the arrival of the first participant. Double check the room arrangement. Is it appropriate for the size of the group and for the scheduled activities? Make any needed adjustments. Pass out materials needed for the day and test the technology to make sure it is working properly. You might take a few moments to review your lesson one last time. Also, pray throughout the room asking for God's presence and guidance. Make sure your room is set and ready to go before the first participant arrives.

Warmly greet each participant as he or she enters the classroom and keep an eye on the time. Though you may not want to begin class with only a few people present, when the scheduled start time is at hand—begin your class! Starting on time sends the message that timeliness is important and encourages all participants to arrive on time for future classes. If someone arrives late, do not stop your instruction to repeat previously presented information. Continue with the lesson, and save reminders and updates for the end of class.

Because schedules are full and lives are busy, there may be participants who cannot attend every class or whose schedule forces them to be late every time. Invite class members to let you know if such a situation exists for them. This will allow time to make advance preparations so absent class members will not miss important information and latecomers can join the class without disrupting instruction.

During Class

Let all things be done decently and in order.
1 Corinthians 14:40 (KJV)

Keeping track of the time will also be necessary while you are teaching your lesson. Setting a predetermined amount of time for each class activity will help you maintain a consistent flow of instruction and ensure you have enough time for each planned activity. Think about how much time you will need for fellowship, lesson study, prayer, discussion and other activities. Use your identified time frames as a guide as you move through the class period. If your class is one hour long, your class routine might look something like this:

2 minutes Welcome and announcements
5 minutes Praise and worship
3 minutes Prayer
4 minutes Lesson review or brief icebreaker activity related to the day's topic
3 minutes Lesson introduction
35 minutes Presentation of lesson content with Scripture reading and discussion
5 minutes Life application challenge
3 minutes Prayer requests and closing prayer

For best results, chunk your lesson content by presenting key information in eight- to ten-minute segments. For example, sharing a memorable story followed by a brief discussion, reading Scripture, and participating in a reflective activity with a partner will provide multiple ways for class members to relate to the day's topic.

You will need to make decisions in real time as you implement your lesson in order to keep your instruction focused and on track. Stick to your routine, but keep your lesson moving by integrating surprises throughout and taking advantage of teachable moments. Help participants stay on task by exercising your facilitation skills. You may have to interrupt and refocus the group when a participant response becomes too lengthy, or to guide the conversation in an unplanned direction if it will lead to new participant understandings.

Even though you have a plan, stay alert, be flexible, and observe and listen to your audience. There will often be occasions when the Holy Spirit takes over and time is not of concern to anyone. On these occasions, let the Spirit flow and use your best judgment as to how to handle the time.

At the End of Class

Just as it is important to begin your class on time, it is also important to end on time. No matter how enjoyable your class may be, participants will expect to be dismissed at the designated end time.

If it appears you will exceed the regular ending time, stop your instruction and make an agreement with the group regarding the anticipated time you will dismiss. Let them know what you would still like to cover and how much time it will take. If they are in agreement with extending the class session, continue until the specified time. As a general courtesy, try not to extend the time beyond five or ten minutes.

Continually observe how participants respond to the various activities you present to gather clues as to what might be most meaningful to them. Select activities that are aligned with your learning outcomes and that can be completed in the time you have available.

Care for Your Crew

Your effectiveness as a teacher will not only be determined by the quality of the lessons you present, but also by the personal connections you make with class members. Build community in your classroom by getting to know participants and providing opportunities for them to connect with one another.

Learn and Remember Names

Starting on the first day of class, make an effort to learn the name of each participant. Provide name tags, if appropriate, and take time to connect with class members before and after class. One helpful way to begin learning more about your participants is to have them introduce themselves on the first day. Introductions might include having participants state their names and a few things about themselves. As each participant shares, you or your assistant can write down the name and other key information for later reference. These notes will aid you in remembering who's who as you connect details about each individual with people and experiences from your own life. During each class, call participants by name and chat with them about specific things shared during class or in their introductions. Show genuine interest and remember what you've heard—this will help you build strong relationships with your class members.

Follow Up

When participants miss several class periods in a row or have sporadic attendance, it will be necessary to follow up with them. Reviewing your attendance roster on a regular basis will help you stay abreast of which participants have attended class consistently and which ones have missed. Poor attendance signals a contact is needed. Such communications should be inviting and pleasant, rather than questioning or accusatory. Let the individual know he or she has been missed, and invite him or her to return for the next class. This is usually all that is needed to encourage continued participation.

Follow Through

As you make follow-up contacts, you may become aware of specific needs or receive requests for prayer or other support. Follow through on these requests, and let participants know what you have done to support them. Keep a notebook or electronic device on hand to note questions and other information on which you may need to follow up. This will help ensure follow-up tasks are not forgotten. Staying on top of such details lets participants know they are valued and viewed as unique contributors in your classroom. These small acts of encouragement will also help you maintain a warm, inviting class culture.

Communicate Between Sessions

Use available technology to stay connected with participants between classes. You might send an email to recap the week's lesson, to share highlights of an upcoming event, or to make class members aware of a change or special need. Once is never enough when sending messages to class participants. A brief announcement in class followed by a detailed email, a call, a text, or a social media post will help ensure class members are aware of plans and changes. Determine the frequency and method that works best for your group, and develop a rhythm for sending periodic communications.

Connecting with and caring for class members are two essentials needed for the success of your class. Your reminders, cheerful notes, and warm follow-up calls will help keep participants engaged and interested.

Celebrate

As mentioned earlier in this guidebook, at some point during your teaching assignment you will want to celebrate successes with your class members. This may come at the end of a lesson series or at a specific time of year if you teach an ongoing class. To make the event a success, enlist the help of your participants to share their special skills and talents. Make the celebration as simple or as elaborate as you like— just remember to pause and celebrate at some time during the instructional cycle.

Celebrations often include reviewing course content, sharing testimonies, and acknowledging class members for their contributions. Distributing certificates of completion or presenting participants with a memento of some sort will make the event extra special. Mementos might include a thoughtful poem or reading, a handcrafted bookmark, or some other inexpensive item that can be cherished for years to come. Make your celebration a true event by including music, food, and time for fun and fellowship. This is also a great time to thank support staff, special helpers, and others who helped make your class a success.

During the celebration, model the importance of continuous spiritual growth and development by expressing the ways the class and the students' input have benefitted you. The group may be surprised to learn you also gained from class discussions.

Each time you interact with your class members, you have the opportunity to plant spiritual seeds and make an impact. By creating engaging lessons, managing your time well, continuously connecting with learners, and celebrating successes, your class will be a meaningful part of participants' Christian education and aid in their spiritual growth and development.

Reflecting and Reporting On Your Work

Ponder the path of your feet; then
all your ways will be sure.
Proverbs 4:26 (ESV)

As your class progresses over time or comes to a close at the end of an instructional cycle, you will automatically begin thinking about ways to improve it. Building a feedback loop into your instructional processes will assist you in enhancing the overall quality of your class and instruction. Gathering feedback will also help you determine if students' spiritual needs are being met.

Gather Participant Feedback

An easy way to gather feedback is to survey class participants. The feedback tool used will depend on the size of the class, the time available, and the kind of information you desire to collect. A hard-copy survey with a few key questions is quite effective and easy to implement. Questions might also be asked using an electronic surveying tool. Many free and low-cost tools are available on the Internet.

Surveys take time to develop and administer; thus, it is important to determine at the start of class what you will do to gather feedback at the end. Have the survey ready long before it is needed in order to ensure this critical action is not overlooked.

Include survey questions that will assist you in gathering information to help improve your class and teaching practices. Questions might focus on:

⇒ what participants gained from participation in the class
⇒ how participants applied or will apply what they have learned
⇒ course logistics (how well the length, time, and location of the class worked)
⇒ your effectiveness (i.e., your knowledge and preparedness as an instructor)
⇒ suggestions participants have for improving the class
⇒ future topics participants would like to study

You will be more likely to receive a response from your class members if you keep the survey short and simple. Hard-copy surveys may be handed out on the final day of class, while electronic surveys might be sent a couple of days before or after the class ends. When sending electronic surveys, give participants ample time to return them and plan to send multiple reminders. If your class is ongoing, strategically schedule times for gathering this information.

Review and Reflect

As your study comes to a close, it is also time to review and summarize attendance records and to take some time to personally reflect on your experience. What do you feel worked well? What seemed to be a challenge? Which aspects of your teaching style were effective? Which ones need more development?

During your reflection you will undoubtedly identify class processes and personal teaching techniques that could use some tweaking. Note specific areas for improvement, and pray for continued insight. Seek out learning opportunities in your church and community that will assist you in developing in these areas.

Don't be too hard on yourself! Teaching is a learning experience in and of itself. Your reflective activities are a natural part of the experience and help ensure continuous improvement.

Summarize and Share Your Experience

Once you have reviewed attendance data and received survey responses from participants, it is time to analyze the information to determine what worked and what might be improved. Use this data along with your personal reflections to create a one- or two-page document that summarizes the experience. The document might include a brief description of the course, dates on which it was held, topic(s) covered, attendance data, successes and challenges, perceived results, and recommendations.

When the document is completed, schedule a time to share it with your ministry leader. Your insights will help inform decisions related to your organization's program of Christian education. The information will also be a great reference for future teachers and leaders.

Reflecting on your work and determining if learning outcomes have been met are critical steps in the instructional cycle. Both of these activities promote continuous improvement and will assist you in operating your class with excellence.

Additional Considerations

Not many of you should become teachers, my fellow believers, because you know that we who teach will be judged more strictly.
James 3:1

There are a few other things to keep in mind as you carry out the duties of teaching. The following are additional considerations important to your work.

Leadership

Teaching is an act of leadership and as with any leadership role, certain standards of conduct are expected. As you interact with others both inside and outside of class, keep your "Bible teacher" title at the forefront of your mind. Whether you are using social media, relaxing at the beach, or attending a celebration at a friend's home, others will observe your speech and actions, and expect you to be an example worthy of emulating. Demonstrating Christian character will have a positive effect on your credibility and will strengthen your impact. Questionable character or behavior will minimize your effectiveness and could require you to be removed from your teaching assignment. Remember to let your inner light shine! Your participants will see your good works, and God will be glorified.

Instructional Challenges

At various times throughout your instruction, you are likely to experience situations that make you feel uncomfortable. You may be challenged by a response from a class member that is scripturally off base or be confronted with a question you do not feel qualified to answer. When such instances arise, remain calm and do not become defensive or argumentative. Instead, welcome these occasions as opportunities to learn. You might gain additional insights by asking other class members to share their opinions. Make a note of the question and their responses, and conduct additional research to find the answer. Seek out church leaders, Bible references, and other resources for additional information on the topic. During your next class you can share the findings with class members. Questioning and debate are a healthy part of the learning process and are a good indication students are learning. Welcome both as growth opportunities for you and for your participants.

Confidentiality

As you serve in the role of Bible teacher, participants may sometimes share information or experiences which surprise or even disturb you. If this happens, be careful to keep your personal thoughts and opinions to a minimum. Listen intently, ask clarifying questions, and share guidance or encouragement from Scripture. If appropriate, invite the individual to pray with you about the concern and seek support from church leaders when needed. Though you may find it difficult to do so, refrain from discussing this information with others. If the situation is so severe that outside help is required, let the class member know the steps you will to take to connect him or her with church or community resources. Your class members must be assured they can openly express personal concerns or information and that the experiences shared will be held in confidence—both now and in the future. Be sure to regularly stress the importance of confidentiality, and consistently model it in your interactions with others.

Absences

Maintaining exceptional attendance is an expectation for every teacher; still, times may arise when you will be unable to keep your commitment due to vacation, illness or some other unforeseen circumstance. Touch base with your ministry leader to determine what steps you should take in the event of an absence. Also, discuss your absence with your assistant. Be proactive by having a plan in place describing what you will do when such instances arise. Identify individuals who might step in when you are away and alert them in advance of the process you will use to inform them and support their work. Try to notify your substitute as early as possible, and go the extra mile to make sure he or she has the information and resources needed to lead the class without difficulty. Having a proactive plan in place will ensure that instructional time is not lost while you are away and that participants have a meaningful learning experience in your absence.

Staying in Touch

Once your study has ended, maintain the connections you have made with class participants. Make an effort to remember names and faces, and greet former class members with a hug and a smile when you see them on the church campus or in the community. Depending on your situation, you might continue to communicate with specific class members via text or email. For example, you could send information regarding other growth opportunities happening at the church or in your community. This will keep class members focused on their spiritual growth and extend your influence beyond the length of your class. By all means, continue to learn, grow, and fellowship together! Check in with former class members often to offer support or to share a word of encouragement. Continue to pray for class members and for needs expressed during class discussions. Of course, if you have provided a meaningful learning experience for your participants, they will want to know when and what you will be teaching next. Thus, it will be time to start the process all over again! Maintain your momentum by sharing information about the next class and encouraging the group's continued participation.

Ending Your Teaching Assignment

As you near the end of each period of study and reflect on your work as a teacher, there may come a time when you feel led to serve in another area. When this happens, notify your leader as soon as possible and work with him or her to identify another teacher so there will not be a break in service. It is also a good idea to inform current participants of your decision. Let the group know you will keep in touch, and encourage class members to stay committed to continued spiritual growth and study. Provide information and resources to the incoming teacher and make yourself available for questions and needed support as he or she gets started. You may experience feelings ranging from joy and relief to guilt and sadness during this time. You will find inner peace as you prayerfully allow the Holy Spirit to guide your decision-making.

Conclusion

Go ye therefore, and teach all nations, baptizing them in the name of the Father, and of the Son, and of the Holy Ghost: Teaching them to observe all things whatsoever I have commanded you: and, lo, I am with you alway, even unto the end of the world. Amen.
Matthew 28:19-20 (KJV)

Your work as a teacher should be off to a great start! Continue to refine your processes and share what you have learned with others. Polish your craft by trying new teaching strategies, and challenge yourself by targeting a broader audience or focusing on more difficult topics. Take time to observe other teachers in action, and continue to pray, read, and study to build your Bible knowledge and teaching expertise.

Though you may never know what impact your instruction made in the lives of your class members, you can rest assured the time and energy you expended produced eternal results.

May blessings overtake you as you serve in ministry and influence the spread of the gospel throughout the nations in your generation.

About the Author

Stephanie R. Moss is an inspired creative who has committed her life to the work of teaching and learning. Working as a teacher, trainer, and learning facilitator for over 30 years in the fields of education and organizational development, Stephanie has developed and facilitated hundreds of learning experiences for both adults and children. Combining skills and experiences gained from her professional work with her spiritual gifts, personal experiences and passions, Stephanie uses writing, teaching, and creative expression to inspire victorious Christian living despite one's circumstances.

Stephanie has served in various Christian ministries throughout her lifetime, and currently volunteers as a small group facilitator in women's ministry. Previous areas of Christian service have included outreach leader, vacation Bible school crafts leader and teacher, greeter, and evangelism outreach team member, among others.

A breast cancer survivor, information junkie, and devoted auntie, Stephanie enjoys mentoring youth and young adults, chasing rabbits on the Internet, creating scrappy quilts, crafting, traveling, reading, and enjoying time with family and friends.

Notes

Notes

Notes

Notes

Notes

Notes

Notes

Printed in the United States
By Bookmasters